OLLIE GIVES A HOOT!

Written by Ellen Krawczak

&

Illustrated by Adam Farver

Copyright © Ellen Krawczak

All rights reserved.

ISBN 978-1-62806-239-7

Library of Congress Control Number 2019910284

Published by Salt Water Media
29 Broad Street, Suite 104
Berlin, MD 21811
www.saltwatermedia.com

FOR

MAGGIE AND ZOEY AND ELSIE

AND

LEXI AND AIDAN

"Will you come to my birthday party?" Maggie Monkey asked Ollie Owl.

"I will not," said Ollie. He added grouchily, "I don't like parties. I don't like being with other animals. I prefer to sleep during the day and stay awake at night. I like being alone. So, leave me alone."

Maggie was very patient and she tried again. "Ollie, this is a special birthday for me. I want all my friends to be with me to celebrate. Won't you join us?"

Ollie glared at her. "I don't have friends and I don't want to be with your friends."

"But Ollie," said Maggie, "everyone needs friends."

"Not me," said Ollie. "I'm independent and I like being alone. And," he added, staring at her with his huge eyes, "I don't give a hoot."

Maggie felt sad. She worried about Ollie. She was afraid that he was lonely. He never came to any of the jungle meetings. He didn't like going from tree to tree visiting the other animals. He turned his beak down at pot luck dinners. He didn't celebrate holidays. He wasn't mean, but he wasn't friendly either.

ZoZo Zebra was Maggie's best friend. She knew that Maggie had invited Ollie to the party and that he said "no." So, she tried.

"Please, Ollie," ZoZo said. "This party is important to Maggie. Stop thinking only of yourself. Please come." Then she wiggled her stripes just to make sure that she had Ollie's attention.

"No and no," said Ollie emphatically. "I won't come. Not now, not ever. I don't give a hoot. Go away and stop bothering me."

ZoZo sighed and went home She had tried.

Lennie Lion also tried.

By then, Ollie was getting angry. "Why are you bothering me? You are cutting into my sleep time." He spread his huge wings and flapped them up and down.

The wind from the wings ruffled Lennie's mane. "Hey," Lennie roared. "Stop that! You are messing up my mane."

Ollie huffed, "I don't care about a party. I don't give a hoot. I just want to go to sleep. Now get out of here."

Robin Red Breast and Billie Bluejay also tried to reason with Ollie.

"Listen to me," Robin said. "Sometimes we all do things that we don't want to do. We do them to make someone else happy. To put a smile on someone's face. To let them know that we care." Robin smiled prettily at Ollie.

"Please come to the party, Ollie. It would mean so much to Maggie."

Ollie scowled at her and Billie. "Do you think that I care? Do you think that I give a hoot?" He swept one of his massive wings back and forth. It almost knocked Robin and Billie from their branch.

"Well, I never," Billie started to say.

"Forget it," said Robin sadly. "He's not going to change. You heard him. He just doesn't give a hoot."

Maggie Monkey and ZoZo Zebra planned Maggie's party. It would be in the clearing on the soft moss. Everyone would make a special dish to contribute to the birthday dinner. ZoZo liked to bake and she would make a birthday cake. Ali Alligator would decorate it and Katie Kangaroo would bring it to the party in her pouch.

Jeff Giraffe would put balloons and decorations up in the trees.

Freddie Frog and his band "The Croakers" would play music throughout the late afternoon and early evening.

It was going to be a wonderful party.

Soon the date came. Maggie Monkey was so excited. She had been looking forward to a birthday party all year. Last year's party was canceled because of strong storms. But today the weather was perfect.

She met up with ZoZo Zebra and they washed themselves by the river. She then brushed her fur and ZoZo Zebra counted her stripes to make sure that she had the same amount as yesterday.

In the late afternoon, the animals started arriving in the clearing.

Jeff Giraffe had done a wonderful job of stringing balloons and flowers and little lights in the trees. It looked like a fairy land.

Bernie Bear and Lenny Lion had set up a big picnic table and the talented Jen Jaguar had made a birthday banner.

Maggie Monkey was very happy. She was so grateful that she had so many caring friends.

Freddie Frog and his band, The Croakers, played music and all the animals danced.

Even the old grandpa, Scott Sea Turtle, made an appearance.

Ollie was not happy. The sounds of the music drifted through the trees waking him. He woke up grouchy. Late afternoon was for sleeping, not for partying. *I did not want to go to that party he complained and now that party has come to me.* He could smell the odors of food being roasted over the fire. He could hear animals singing. The ground shook with animals dancing. *I wish I didn't have such good hearing*, he thought. *I feel like I'm right at that party.* *Bah humbug*, he said to himself and then he said it out loud. "Bah humbug!"

Ollie had great hearing. He could hear the music quiet down and he could hear the crinkling of paper as Maggie Monkey unwrapped her gifts. He could hear all the oohs and ahhs as Maggie Monkey opened present after present. Everyone was talking and sounding happy. Ollie became angrier and angrier. *All I want is to be left alone in peace. Is that too much to ask?* He was unhappy that he could hear everything going on at the party, even though it was miles away.

But then he heard a click. Ollie stood very still. He thought he knew what that click meant. He had heard it before. It was a rifle and it meant danger. And, then he heard the men. He sensed there were two of them. Hunters. He heard them walking very softly through the jungle. He heard them whispering.

"What luck that all the animals are in one place," said one hunter.

"It certainly will be easy not to have to chase them," said the other.

The first hunter said, "Just what we want for dinner."

Ollie stiffened. Maggie Monkey and the others were not his friends, but the jungle was their home and they deserved to live there safely.

Ollie needed to warn them. He could fly to the clearing where Maggie Monkey and her friends were, but that would take too long. *How, how do I warn them?* And, then he remembered that he could hoot. He always thought of himself as the strong silent type, sitting still, not saying much of anything to anybody. But now was the time for action. He opened his beak and a weak little "hoot" came out. He would have to do better. He tried again and again. He became scared. He could hear the hunters and it sounded like they were getting closer and closer to the party.

He took in a large breath and blew it out. A hoot shrieked along the sky. First one and then another and then another.

Maggie Monkey was opening her last present when she heard a sound. "What was that?" she asked.

ZoZo Zebra had heard it, too.

Jeff Giraffe stood up very tall. "Everyone be quiet," he said softly.

Then it came again, and it got louder and louder. Ollie was hooting, strongly and repeatedly. "Ollie's in trouble," Maggie said. "We have to go see what's wrong."

The animals crashed through the jungle trying to get to Ollie. Some ran and some flew and some swung from tree to tree. Everyone was scared. Something terrible must be happening to Ollie for him to hoot so loudly and so continuously. The friends reached Ollie's tree. "Go, scatter!" he shouted.

"There are hunters in the jungle and they are near by. Everyone run in a different direction. Go," he pleaded. The animals ran and they hid. Ali Alligator slithered into the water. Freddie Frog hid on a lily pad. Bernie Bear went into his den. Jeff Giraffe tried to blend into the trees. All the animals waited silently in their hiding places.

Ollie could hear the angry voices of the hunters.

They were furious that the animals had been warned. "That awful owl made such a commotion that the animals took off," said the first hunter.

"Let's try to find him," said the second.

"Good idea," said the first.

The hunters could not see Ollie who stood very still on his branch.

"I don't hear him anymore," said the first hunter. "It's getting dark," said the second. "The jungle is no place to be at night. Let's go home."

After the hunters left, all the animals gathered around Ollie's tree. They called out to him and asked if he was okay. Ollie flew down to the ground and joined them. He told them that he had been scared but that now he was okay. He looked around and saw such kind faces. He saw animals who cared about him. He saw that they were willing to help him and to help each other.

"Thank you for warning us," said Maggie Monkey.

"You saved our lives," ZoZo Zebra added.

"You are our hero," said the friends.

Ollie's beak quavered. He cleared his throat. "I do not want to be a hero," Ollie said. "I want to be a friend. Is it too late to be a friend?"

The animals circled around Ollie.

"It's never too late to make a new friend." Maggie Monkey said, "Being my friend is the best birthday present you can give me."

Ollie still lives in his tree. Every morning, before he goes to sleep, he hoots to wake up his friends. In the evening, when he wakes up, he hoots again to let everyone know that it is time to go to sleep. He is looking forward to having all his friends come to his birthday party next month!

CPSIA information can be obtained
at www.ICGtesting.com
Printed in the USA
LVHW020931210120
644250LV00012B/604